D1308351

Life Under the Sea
Parrotfish

by Cari Meister

Bullfrog Books

Ideas for Parents and Teachers

Bullfrog Books let children practice reading informational text at the earliest reading levels. Repetition, familiar words, and photo labels support early readers.

Before Reading

- Ask the child to think about ocean animals. Ask: What do you think a parrotfish is?

- Look at the picture glossary together. Read and discuss the words.

Read the Book

- "Walk" through the book and look at the photos. Let the child ask questions. Point out the photo labels.

- Read the book to the child, or have him or her read independently.

After Reading

- Prompt the child to think more. Ask: Is a parrotfish more like a fish or a parrot? Why do you think it is called a parrotfish?

Bullfrog Books are published by Jump!
5357 Penn Avenue South
Minneapolis, MN 55419
www.jumplibrary.com

Library of Congress Cataloging-in-Publication Data

Meister, Cari, author.
  Parrotfish / by Cari Meister.
    pages cm. — (Life under the sea)
  Audience: 5-8.
  Audience: Grade K to 3.
  Summary: "This photo-illustrated book for early readers tells about the physical features of parrotfish, what they eat, and how they protect themselves. Includes picture glossary" — Provided by publisher.
  Includes bibliographical references and index.
  ISBN 978-1-62031-100-4 (hardcover) —
  ISBN 978-1-62496-167-0 (ebook)
  1. Parrotfishes — Juvenile literature. I. Title.
II. Series: Bullfrog books. Life under the sea.
QL638.S3M45 2015
597'.7—dc23
                                        2013042378

Series Editor: Rebecca Glaser
Series Designer: Ellen Huber
Book Designer: Anna Peterson
Photo Researcher: Kurtis Kinneman

Photo Credits: AHDesignConcepts/iStock, 20–21; aquapix/Shutterstock, 3; Birgitte Wilms/Minden Pictures/Corbis, 14; Chad Zuber/Shutterstock, 9, 23tl; Dave Fleetham/Design Pics/Corbis, 8; Dr. Ajay Kumar Singh/Shutterstock, 6 inset, 23ml; Dreamframer| Dreamstime.com, 22; Georgie Holland/age fotostock/ SuperStock, 12–13, 23mr; PAUL SUTHERLAND/National Geographic Creative, 16–17, 23br; Reinhard Dirscherl/ Getty Images, 18–19; Rich Carey/Shutterstock, cover, 5, 15; Richard Carey|Dreamstime.com, 1, 24; Universal Images Group/SuperStock, 6–7; Visuals Unlimited/ Corbis, 10–11; Vlad61/Shutterstock, 4, 10–11, 23tr

Printed in the United States of America at Corporate Graphics, in North Mankato, Minnesota.
3-2014
10 9 8 7 6 5 4 3 2 1

Table of Contents

A Fish of Many Colors

Look at the reef.

What is that?

It is a parrotfish!

It has big teeth.
What do they look like?
A parrot's beak!

beak

6

teeth

7

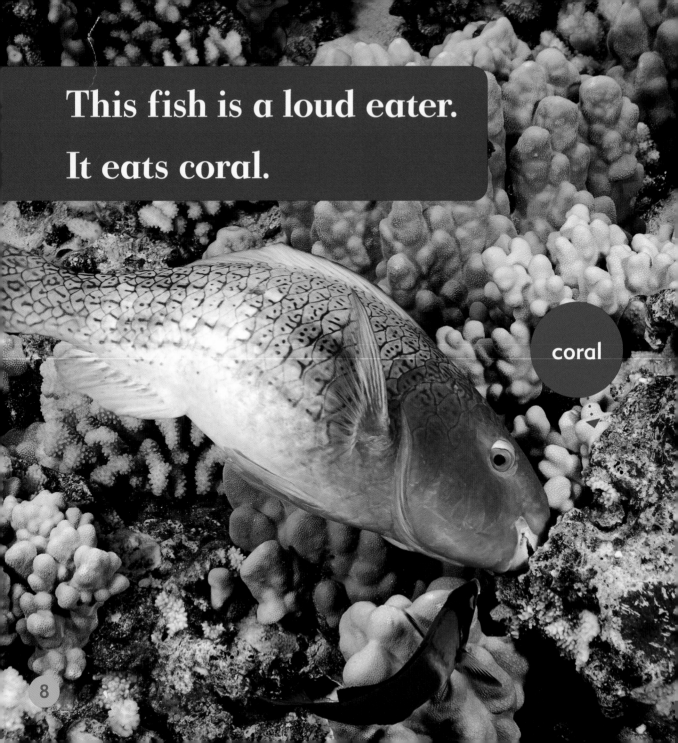

This fish is a loud eater.

It eats coral.

coral

algae

It likes the algae inside.
Yum!

sand

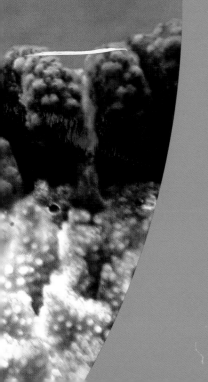

The coral is crushed.

It comes out of the fish.

Now it is sand.

These fish live in schools.
They make a lot of sand.
Wow!

They change as they grow.
A young fish is dull.

A grown-up has lots of colors.
Pretty!

A parrotfish makes
a sleeping bag.

He uses slime.

It is sticky.

It comes off his skin.

slime

17

The slime smells bad.

Yuck!

Other fish do not like it.

They stay away.

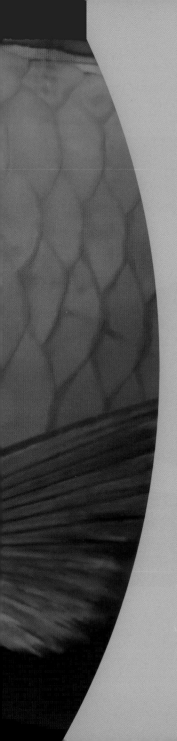

A parrotfish goes to sleep.

His eyes stay open.

Sleep well, fish!

Parts of a Parrotfish

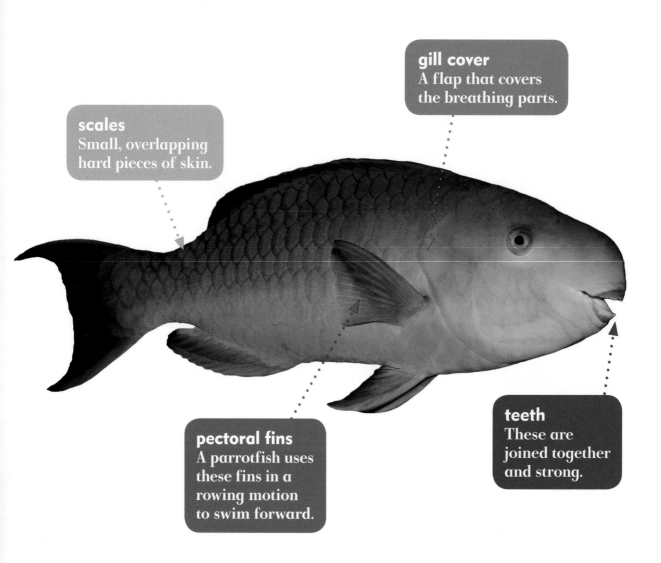

gill cover
A flap that covers the breathing parts.

scales
Small, overlapping hard pieces of skin.

pectoral fins
A parrotfish uses these fins in a rowing motion to swim forward.

teeth
These are joined together and strong.

Picture Glossary

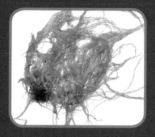
algae
Small plants with no roots or stems that grow in or near water.

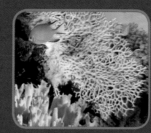
reef
A strip of coral in shallow ocean water.

beak
The hard, horny parts of a bird's mouth.

school
A group of fish that lives together in the sea.

coral
Hard skeletons of small sea animals.

slime
A sticky, gooey fluid that a parrotfish makes.

Index

To Learn More

Learning more is as easy as 1, 2, 3.

1) Go to www.factsurfer.com

2) Enter "parrotfish" into the search box.

3) Click the "Surf" button to see a list of websites.

With factsurfer.com, finding more information is just a click away.